TILL THE TIDE
AN ANTHOLOGY OF MERMAID POETRY

Sundress Publications
www.sundresspublications.com

Till the Tide: An Anthology of Mermaid Poetry
Copyright © 2015

Edited by Trista Edwards
trista@sundresspublications.com
Designed by Rhonda Lott
rhonda@sundresspublications.com

This book is set in Baskerville Old Face.

ISBN: 978-1-939675-14-9

TILL THE TIDE

AN ANTHOLOGY OF MERMAID POETRY

Edited by Trista Edwards

CONTENTS

EDITOR'S NOTE

Anais Nin once wrote, "I must be a mermaid, Rango. I have no fear of depths and a great fear of shallow living." The quote, spoken by the female protagonist Djuna, is from Nin's 1950 novel *The Four-Chambered Heart,* a narrative based on her real-life love affair with Peruvian poet, Gonzalo Morè. This quote has always resonated with me, as it has become a philosophy on how I wish to live my life—ever-transient and fearless, a mermaid. I have always loved mermaids. As a child, I would spread the largest quilt I could find on the floor of the living room, and then, positioning myself just so only my legs touched the fabric, I would roll. I would roll up in the quilt until I had wound myself a tight, cotton fin. I would lounge about in my fin, reading, watching movies, playing with my dolls, all day. As child, I loved the transformation, the hybridity of my own body. It was hard not to look down at my long blanket fin that stretched well beyond my feet and not feel powerful. Completely in awe of the difference of my own appearance, it was this tail that could take me to those inexplicable depths, and although just a young girl, I, like Djuna, felt intrepid.

As an adult, I have become even more fascinated by mermaids and all their symbolic complexities. I love their femininity, their sensuality, their mystery, their villainy, and not only their power but their power by voice. As a female poet, I am unabashedly drawn to that particular trait—the power of the female voice. In poetry, the mermaid as symbol and muse for verse extends to Dickinson, Yeats, Hughes, Eliot, Keats, Homer, Neruda, Rich, Atwood, Shakespeare, and Milton, just to name a few. Of course, "mermaid" has become an amalgamation, the flagship word, for siren, water nymph, sea witch, seductress, femme fatal, and enchantress. And if you scour the entries in the

Oxford English Dictionary, you will continue to find glosses that extend to mentions of Animalia (manatee or "sea-cow"), a prostitute, an aquaholic (a "woman who is at home in the water"), and yes, even a poet. Her likeness bleeds across cultures and through various legends to include figures such as Lorelei, Melusine, Selkie, Pincoya, and Rusalka. Her definition is as fluid at the sea she hails from. Although, despite the slight differences in all these cultures, figures, and stories, one element remains the same—her mesmerizing voice that leads you to either ruin or transformation. Once you hear her, your life will forever be changed.

The poets featured in this anthology share work that in some way utilizes the figure of mermaid. You will find her legend revisited and reconfigured, at times evoking the aforementioned figures or the poet's own contemporary interpretation of what it is to be this songstress. The title of this anthology borrows its name from Emily Dickinson's "I started Early – Took my Dog" in which the speaker begins:

> I started Early – Took my Dog –
> And visited the Sea –
> The Mermaids in the Basement
> Came out to look at me –
>
> And Frigates – in the Upper Floor
> Extended Hempen Hands –
> Presuming Me to be a Mouse –

And then later, a few stanzas further along:

> But no Man moved Me – till the Tide
> Went past my simple Shoe –
> And past my Apron – and my Belt
> And past my Boddice – too –

And made as He would eat me up –
As wholly as a Dew

Opon a Dandelion's Sleeve –
And then – I started – too –

In this poem, the female speaker begins a journey to the beach with her canine companion and finds solace in her imagined mermaids that rise up from their metaphorical house. The poem turns though as the sea becomes personified as man, Poseidon, and threatens to engulf the speaker. Throughout the poem, the speaker oscillates between comfort, fear, loss, and unity. Her transformation through these qualities is apparent, and while the sea possesses a still surface at times, below there exists the possibility of something much more sinister. And with her traditionally split tail and fused body, the mermaid, too, represents a powerful, bifurcated nature–sanctuary and danger; human and myth; wrath and mercy. So whether you view the mermaid as a harbinger or a cruel seductress of the sea, a villainous man-eater or a matron of wild freedom, a feminine warrior or the epitome of unbridled sexuality, she is powerful nonetheless. My hope is that whichever way, you leave this book with a sense of transformation.

I would like to express my gratitude to all the contributors gathered here in this anthology for their beautiful words and their shared mer-love. I thank my teachers and mentors who although they may not have known of my strange obsession have shaped my love, appreciation, and understanding of poetry and literature over the years: Chad Davidson, Bruce Bond, Greg Fraser, Alison Umminger, Meg Person, Corey Marks, and Margaret Mitchell. I thank my family, especially my mum, who, when I was five, brought home a VHS copy of Disney's *The Little Mermaid* and

3

started my twenty-five years and counting fascination with Ariel and her many variations. I thank Aaron Wolin, the man who tells me every day I am the most beautiful mermaid in the sea. Finally, I thank you, reader, for picking up this book. I hope that in reading these works you will find inspiration to take to the deep and overcome the tide.

I started Early - Took my Dog -
And visited the Sea -
The Mermaids in the Basement
Came out to look at me -

—Emily Dickinson

How to Tell if You're a Mermaid: A Quiz

You drowned one day:
a.) when you fell off a dock
b.) at your abusive lover's house
c.) and you think he may have pushed you,
    but it doesn't change the fact–
d.) you inhaled sharp salt that pierced
    your nostrils and weighted
    down your lungs

He didn't save you because:
a.) he was busy getting drunk
b.) he wanted you to die
c.) it made him feel like a man to push you
    with one hand while holding a beer in the other
d.) he knew his slurred cuss would be the last sound
    you'd ever hear

You didn't fight it since:
a.) you had nothing to live for
b.) the water embraced you
    in a way you had forgotten
c.) you're a Pisces and always felt
    water was your home
d.) all of the above

You came to love it when:
a.) the world went black
    though your eyes were
    wide open
b.) your body became a sodden shell
c.) you became a mermaid for submitting

to the sea

d.) A and C only

And Then the Swim

The sea, the water, the glass breaking.
Towers, towns underneath.
Underneath the waves can't be waves.

There must be fish to keep her
company and in the waters
when she is really ready to go.

Add more water to the tail.
Show her waist lassoed
in seaweed, in brine. Blame Barnum.

The hair can't be pinned,
down it covers what is human,
female. Down it skates around her face.

Save what you can of your ship,
the wood piles you didn't see coming,
didn't hear until that mouth opened,
human and then the swim, fish.

Return to Mermaid

I returned to her from overseas,
    unable to dunk away the desert
        sands and unwashable stains.
She waited for me in the trailer
décor, a thrift-store museum
    of mismatched boat relics, walls
        lined with buoys, fish mounted
    on the walls with mouths agape,
posters of famous ocean tragedies.
    The carpeting was a polluted green
        sea and the overcast stucco ceiling
    a single cloud mass observing us.
My mermaid nested in the depth
    and depression of me, a glimpse
        of the man I drowned in fatigues.

On Loving a Solider

If I knew you when the desert was
nothing but a turquoise sea
I would rub you against me like a silver fish
with puckered lips and slippery skin
or squeeze you tightly with violet tentacles
until you remembered how to breathe.
I would cover my breasts with stars
and tickle your chest with coiled hair
or carry you home on my slick, strong fin
if you were too tired or lost your way.

But I met you under bone-dry sky
where the earth is scorched and hard
and you cannot stop leaking sand from your eyes
as you try to forget all that you've done.
You lick your cracked lips as I play my guitar
but you can no longer conjure the tune
and your body goes limp when I try to remind you
how high you can feel when you sing along.
There once was a day when you simply knew
how to open a shell, how to wiggle your toes
but your heart is parched and empty now
so I lie in the light and let you go.

Dearest

Although everything has passed
over a dark sea, over bronze
urchins with their hands
in their zippers, nothing
has passed through me
without your face on it.
Garters sign cursive
in the name of Magdalene,
whom you would have
grown bitter and cold
against twenty-dollar bills.
You never write, and the road
is a lonesome one.
All right, I think,
and pulse incurably
and hang on a hula-hoop
with damp panties, misted
before stage by a spray-bottle
filled with gin. We call this love.

Small Burdens

You can complain about rats as loudly
as you wish. You can point out their long whiskers
and unsanitary feet, bemoan the noises

that taint your dreams. Whine about stolen
food: half nibbled crackers, gored melons.

Rant about the ravens, the entrails they scatter
around your yard, like confetti. The neighborhood
children know not to enter. Death
lingers on your telephone wire.

But do not bother lodging a complaint against
the mermaids that throw parties at midnight
in the ocean at the end of your lawn. Cheap white
wine bottles dot the shoreline,

but do not swear. They can hear you.
They can do much worse than that.

The Homemade Mermaid

The Homemade Mermaid is top half pimply teenager, bottom half tuna. This does not make for a comely silhouette, and the fact that her bits are stitched together with black fishing wire only makes the combo more gruesome. The Homemade Mermaid floods *Mermag*'s "Ask Serena" column with postcards that read, "O why not half salmon or half koi?" signed Frankenmaid. Sure, she's got the syndrome—loves her weird-eyed maker who began his experiments with Barbies and goldfish in a basement years ago—but she does sometimes wish he'd picked her prettier sister and left her tanning on tinfoil in the yard. When he lugs the Homemade Mermaid to the ocean, she always comes swimming back, propelled only by her arms. She really hasn't reconciled with that tail. The next day he can usually be cajoled into playing a game of All Girl—they tuck her tail in a tank behind her and her human half sits pertly at a desk. Whether she's playing secretary or schoolgirl, the game always ends when the mixture of glue and glitter that he's still perfecting for her tail sparkles gets stuck in the tank ventilation system and the engine coughs to a stop. She sighs as he scoops out the glittery sludge. Tonight again he'll serve her algae with anchovies and she won't complain. The one time he brought her fries—delicious fries—she took them as if in a trance, and dipped them, two at a time into the ketchup. The shared memory sprang to both their faces—two severed legs, blood everywhere, his hand gripping the saw.

14

The Backyard Mermaid

The Backyard Mermaid slumps across the birdbath, tired of fighting birds for seeds and lard. She hates those fluffed-up feathery fish imitations, but her hatred of the cat goes fathoms deeper. That beast is always twining about her tail, looking to take a little nip of what it considers a giant fish. Its breath smells of possible friends. She collects every baseball or tennis ball that flies into her domain to throw at the creature, but it advances undeterred, even purring. To add further insult to injury it has a proper name, Furball, stamped on a silver tag on its collar. She didn't even know she had a name until one day she heard the human explaining to another one, "Oh that's just the backyard mermaid." Backyard Mermaid, she murmured, as if in prayer. On days when there's no sprinkler to comb through her curls, no rain pouring in glorious torrents from the gutters, no dew in the grass for her to nuzzle with her nose, not even a mud puddle in the kiddie pool, she wonders how much longer she can bear this life. The front yard thud of the newspaper every morning. Singing songs to the unresponsive push mower in the garage. Wriggling under fence after fence to reach the house four down which has an aquarium in the back window. She wants to get lost in that sad glowing square of blue. Don't you?

The Inside Out Mermaid

The Inside Out Mermaid is fine with letting it all hang out—veins, muscles, the bits of fat at her belly, her small grey spleen. At first her lover loves it—with her organs on the outside, she's the ultimate open book. He can pump her lungs like two bellows and make her gasp; ask her difficult questions and study the synapses firing in her brain as she answers to see if she's lying; poke a pleasure center in the frontal lobe and watch her squirm. Want to tug on her heartstrings? No need for bouquets or sad stories about his childhood. He just plucks a pulmonary vein and watch the left ventricle flounder. But before long, she starts to sense that her lover, like all the others before him, is getting restless. This is usually when she starts showing them her collections—the basket of keys from all over the world, the box of zippers with teeth of every imaginable size—all chosen to convey a sense of openness. As a last resort, she'll even read out loud the entries from her diary about him to him. But eventually he'll become convinced she's hiding things from him and she is. Her perfect skin. Her long black hair. Her red mouth, never chapped from exposure to sun or wind and how she secretly loves that he can't touch her here or here.

Steve Shelby and the Mermaid

He surfaced from blank, blue fields, a prize on his hairy forearm.
He laid it on sand
that clotted its scales. He planned to love it, I could tell. Fish
from the waist down. Last
month, I sank into his lap, belted his arm around my waist, his
fingers busy in my coils
of hair, decoding, decoding. Over his shoulder, she smiled at me,
with that mouth made
for smiling. Those sunning lips. That must have cooled him. He
bound her wrists with
shiny black twine, began clubbing her from head to tail. And I, in
death's thick pit, was
suddenly outside myself, not saving her.

Sea Witch I: Self-Employed

I work from home,
a business model built
on repurposed bones
so many drowned men
buried in my backyard,
why not make use of them?
You may find me
monstrous. I am not
so squeamish.
All my love potions
come with warning labels,
the price too high,
no guarantee.
Don't blame me
if business is brisk, see
all the pretty ones lined up,
begging to pay
the premium. Believe me,
I am not lacking
in compassion.
I warn them all.
Not once, but twice.
But no one ever listens
to me.

Sea Witch II: Split

A poisonous scrim covers me
salty as sea air, my sand-dusted skin
metallic, glistening, enticing enough
when I was young, still

a century's worth of lovers
and not one ever managed
to lick off the stinging slime.

I've grown attached to it,
this phosphorescent afterbirth
lighting up my limbs

> (I carved them myself
> from my own scaled tail,
> how else does one learn?)

These days I only shine at night
if anyone ever cared
to look. No one does.

Good thing too.
I burn the tongue
like the skin of a tree frog.
Most spit me out quickly
if they know what's good for them.

The Little Mermaid at the Aquatic Arts Academy (AAA)

Accordion music or maybe an arrow-to-the-heart
ballad would be an apt soundtrack to my potholed

career path. Take, for example, that stint at a reception
desk. I called it entry level traffic guard, although Ms.

Employment Counselor described the role as voice-and-
face-of-the-corporation. Turned out my whole

gestalt was a mismatch. I smiled like a Cheshire cat
hovering over an open tin of caviar as documented on

instant replay video. So, no surprise, I was summarily
jettisoned from that corporate ship. Digging in my castoff

knapsack of talents, I unpacked that latent dream:
Lounge Singer. You know, sitting sexy on a piano like

Madonna as Breathless Mahoney in silver lamé coaxing no-
nonsense Dick Tracy, the hunky Mr. Beatty, to let his body

oooh, go with the flow, baby. My sultry voice, however
promising in the shower, sank in the noisy jungle

quicksand of lounge chatter and clinking ice cubes.
Rescue came at last when an undercover mermaid

support group intervened and splish, splash
threw me into the saltwater pool at the Triple A.

Underwater, a vortex whirled away my vocational
vampires. The Academy hired me to teach Senior Swim,

Water Baby Level Two and Marathon Swim Skills for
X-treme Athletes. We swam, old and jelly-limbed

young, novice and expert, immersed in that fluid
zone where body becomes buoyant vessel.

Advisory Letter: Little Mermaid to Errant Lover

Astrologically, our destiny was to float the ocean of bliss.
Both of us water signs, skilled at navigating life's erratic

currents. Me, Cancer, flirty and friendly as a SeaWorld
dolphin performing for a hunk of raw flesh. You, Scorpio,

elusive and electric as the eels in the saltwater tank at
Four Treasures in Chinatown where Mr. Yee mixes

Gimlets for Lovers (adding one tiny drop of bitters), their
house specialty. In my experience, love needs secret

ingredients. I'm a fingers-crossed gal who wears a lucky
jackalope foot on a lanyard so I can stroke its soft

karmic powers in times of need. Like now, reviewing
laundry lists of your deep-water indiscretions.

Mermaids (you didn't know?) live for 300 years, so run the
numbers. Singlehandedly I could go through a veritable

ocean of men which is likely to earn me poison
pen letters and a cache of flame mail despite

quantum meruit. Fellini said it was easier to be faithful to
restaurants than a woman. I'd edit the gender to man.

Scorpio man, eel man, here's da plan. I'll book our old
table at Four Treasures where my guy, Mr. Yee, will

undertake plying you with gimlets, the double bitters version. Their side effects—print too fine to read—include

weeping a Pacific Ocean of remorse. Till then, expect all future horoscopes and fortune cookies to read:

Yada, yada, yada. Cinch up your Speedo. If you wanna play Zeus, you gotta synchronize your strokes. Call me.

[At last, to be identified!]

A dirigible powered us through the first leg,
    traversing snow-capped mountains where goats
leapt from crags, and men with wrinkled
    apple faces looked up, pointed.

Smiling
    to cold air, I slept under a bear skin,
        touched your lips in the night.

    On our pleasant soap
bubble journey, we dropped baskets down
    each morning, hooked meats, cheeses;
    in later weeks, nothing. Still, we took notes,

detailing the weather conditions, the migrating
    elk numbers and their steady decrease.
Northward by cracked compass,
    the sleet sheeting the balloon drove us low, then lower—

In time we cut through the ice, sank
fathoms into the sea, chaperoned by seals
    that are not mermaids at all.

Else you think this a hoax, know my hand—
down here still—please send help.

The Sailor Visits The Mermaid at Weeki Wachee

The sailor promised her things: gems
she couldn't get from the ocean, a chance
to travel the land, a clawfoot bathtub
where she could still, from time to time,
put on her tail. If she agreed, he told her,
his small blue eyes wrinkling, life would change
forever, for better, right away. His teeth,
she observed as he talked, were straight,
but soft at the edges, the bottoms almost round.
The front two bound together, it seemed,
by something foreign, a strip of resin, or maybe
plastic? "It's wood," he tells her, tapping
the little space with his knuckle. Now
that he's said it, she can't stop staring,
fixed on the tiny part of him that's not real.

Before Weeki Wachee

Before her life as a mermaid, she had other
lives, other jobs. Once, she managed a pizza shop,
wore a red checkered apron and learned
to toss dough in the air lightly like a beach ball.
Before that, she clerked at a motel, worked
the check out desk, had to wear black pumps
every day. For a brief period – her favorite –
she was the Sunkist girl, walking along the beach
barefoot, samples of the orange soda balanced
on her right hand. The uniform was different
than a mermaid's: a pair of denim cut-offs, painted
toenails, an orange tank top hugging her flesh. They hired
her for her breasts, round, big, and young, and for that other
thing about her – the shine they couldn't describe.
People loved her. At the beach, men and women
circled her like bugs around a light, waited
minutes before asking for their ration from her tray,
their tiny part of her.

La Pincoya

She arrived from Chile already christened with a name, with a story of the ocean in her cypress keel and a small woodstove like a salt scrubbed heart. The man tells the woman the myth of Pincoya, who when dancing the shore, her face to the sea, foretells an abundance of fish, or her face to the mountains, a season of scarcity. The woman faces the man who stokes the tiny stove with bits of driftwood that momentarily resemble toy horses or deer or rabbits, and the porthole circles contain the mountain's trees, the cathedral groves where light scarce grows.

The Afterlife of Agua Mala

> *Man-of-Wars or Agua Mala, are covered in venom-filled nematocysts*
> *used to paralyze and kill fish and other small creatures. Beware,*
> *even dead Man-of-Wars washed up on shore can deliver a sting.*
> —National Geographic

Waves cargo her blue poisonous thread of a soul
over the Sea of Cortez, and Agua Mala arrives—already dead.

Near the gold-flecked shore, I wade gleeful and far from home
not knowing the clear bubble of Agua Mala's last breath hobbles

the water's surface like an old beggar asking, *who will remember me?*
I cry in disbelief as if she'd been an ever-sickly grandmother

finally passing away and leaving a graceful, dotted blue ink trail
from my thigh, behind my knee, the muscles of my calf made numb.

Oh, I fight her tooth and nail, Agua Mala's saline sting, and yet
the harder I kick the waves, the tighter her string of fire pearls

bead into my flesh and stitch a network of elegant welts
over the thin skin of my fattened kneecap, my swelling shin.

She, like an old warship and the smoky tendrils of each buckshot,
leaves poison traces in the blood of the living, those swimmers

who want to believe the flecks of churning fool's gold
are the ocean's way of compensating for Agua Mala's venom.

For several days I limp. I study the tangle of shiny welts,
but there's no sense in it, no glossolalia to explain God's aim—

it's just circumstance: a life, a death, a hundred stings.
And soon I board a plane for home, a landscape draped in moss,

where Agua Mala's last breath dwindles through my blood.

The Wedding of Cecyl and Otter

Everyone knew it was a match made somewhere between heaven
and the Pacific Ocean. Where the fins of angels transform
ocean swells into wedding veils of translucent greens and browns.

We gathered there like Man-of-Wars in a raft of glinting seaweed.
Above the head of every guest a seagull flew in corkscrew patterns,
and their calls reeled out for miles causing fishermen great confusion.

Cecyl appeared from the south, a great wind lifting her hair, her hands
each holding half an abalone shell. She came to playful Otter—who
never for a moment took the wedding seriously—and emptied her hands.

This was all there was: empty hands and flying shells. We all let go
handfuls of sea salt, streamers of bull kelp, underwater squeals,
the language of Flying Fish translated into warm blooded celebration.

Dusk deepened in the East and to our West waves pulled down the sun.
We never saw them go, only what they left: phosphorescent wake
leading from their wedding night to places too dark and beautiful for fear.

Mermaid Time Share

Beneath contempt she was,
a jilter of bandana'd pirates and Mesoamericans.
Her gossamer heart pumped endorphin-laced
excuses even dimestore rapscallions
saw right through.

Mysterious apprentice she was,
attending exorcism night school
where her undeclared major
in banana republic marketing
thrust her onto a crystal meth archipelago
with one model unit never traded, never sold.

Carotids like wax she had, unrelieved
when industrialization crept up her skirted
island retreat.

When a Mermaid Comes Undone

Inconsequential shells—sometimes a chipped agate—
pay them daily to the gods of hazard.

Stealth is your best suit
to unpucker those drenched lips.

Hide in reef shadow. Avoid
black-clad grief divers who grope after their own hearts.

If compromise swims by, as it will,
up-end that raft of innuendo and guilt.

Don't connive or flutter. Go deep.
If you let it, forgiveness will eventually save you.

Bad Girl Ghazal

Your past life was hardly benign or eligible for the glow of redemption.
Let's ponder your chances for an intervention or the glow of redemption.

Drenched in lavender, you managed an excellent deflowering.
How much synergy was lost begs the undertow of redemption.

The din of each humongous sin after that is one hilarious orchestra.
Nevertheless, each prayer seeks a musical flow of redemption.

Your brand of fun was never even remotely symmetrical.
Cruelty glared, did not share quarters with the slow march of redemption.

At last, though, Girl, wisdom has found you giving and grateful.
Your reward is not sainthood. But it *is* a turn in the vast glow of redemption.

Pantoum

Little girl, your veins are showing through
your skin again. And again I will ignore it.
I will lay you down in the ordinary clover
and resume sex, our routine conspiracy.

Your skin again and again, I will ignore it—
although I can barely stand its blue-pink flush—
and resume. Sex, our routine conspiracy,
tethers me to the slim bent weed of your body

although I can barely stand. Its blue-pink flush
of fish's gills, albino snake's pellucid scales
tether me. To the slim bent weed of your body,
an artist might attribute the vulnerable beauty

of fish's gills, albino snakes' pellucid scales . . .
I am your husband. I can't see things the way
an artist might. Attributing "a vulnerable beauty"
is like a wry poem admiring its own cleverness.

I am your husband; I can't see things the way
I did before I knew you. Now my life
is like a wry poem: admiring its own cleverness,
it alienates the one who reads. I can't remember what

I did before I knew you, now. My life
a deconstructed text. What's the point of writing that
alienates the one who reads? I can't remember. What
can save us from seeing too much?

A deconstructed text—what? Is the point of writing that
our roles are judged irrelevant? Only love
can save us from seeing. Too much
rain has filled the mossy gutters; too many hours

our roles are judged: irrelevant. Only, love
returns me to this house at night, where
rain has filled the mossy gutters. Too many hours
spent feeling thunder rattle the iron bedframe

return me to this house at night, where
I'm like one treading water, mindless,
spent. Feeling thunder rattle the iron bedframe,
I mistake its tremble for my own—

I'm like one treading water, mindless
of the riptide, deadly current so strong
I mistake its tremble. For my own
long sweet strokes in the pale water

of the riptide—deadly current so strong—
pull me out to sea. And hold me
long, sweet. Stroke in the pale water
your mermaid's flesh: you belong here tangled in sea-reeds.

Pull me out to sea and hold me,
little girl. Your veins are showing through
your mermaid's flesh. You belong here. Tangled in sea-reeds,
I will lay you down in this extraordinary clover.

Misconceptions about Mermaids

Madison the mermaid hides
her true self, using a blow dryer
to dry her tail after a long bath.
The year was 1984.[1]
However.
The only acceptable dip is the salt-laden sea;
a mermaid can't find pleasure in a ceramic tub.
Mermaid tails never magically turn into legs. [2]

Little Ariel befriends a singing crustacean,[3]
pines for a world above the sea,
falls for a prince who has two legs.
The year was 1989.[4]
However.
Underwater princes with flippers,
win out over limbs any day.
Mermaids have already found
ways to navigate across hard land

without legs, without magic,
without scripts or screen,
no artificial animation required.
They roam among us. They are here.

---

[1] Daryl Hannah's blonde frame plastered across billboards, buses, and TV screens. She would act opposite Tom Hanks[*] in the romantic comedy *Splash!*

[2] Do we think Pan's goat legs become human legs when he's not on grass? Do we think Centaurs' bottoms become human bottoms when they cross the country border?

[3] Crustaceans have really bad rhythm. The only time they sing is when they get tipsy on squid ink.

[4] The Disney factory animated an old tale about a dangerous deal between a sea hag[**] and a mermaid, and added two eels named Flotsam and Jetsam.

[*] Fun Fact: The mermaid population is one of the few groups who have a disdain for Tom Hanks.

[**] Sea hags don't exist. A kind jellyfish named Ursula DiLaurento received hate mail and death threats until the onset of Mulan.

Breaking in Ice Skates

My feet are trapped inside the white boots,
ankle to toe cast in a cocoon of leather and lacquer,

screws and a set of silver swords. I think of the mermaid
who wanted to be human and how her magical legs

ached with each unsteady step. When I skate, cold wind
whips my face, the ice uncertain as stormy waves.

For weeks this is the routine, laces like fisher's nets,
tied to mangle my young toes, to grant me the gift

of water-walking, of flight in winter's fog. After practice,
blisters bloom across my soles like algae, blood

seeps into socks, into the bathroom rug. This
is my transformation. The slow craft of muscle and bone

into scales more malleable. To forget the pain, I imagine
my skirt spreading to fins in the midst of a scratch spin,

the sequins shimmering to pearls in the toe-loop.
And when I land, when I am done defying gravity,

I think of seafoam and the salty collapse of body to water—
fish women watching me beneath the ice.

Hinged Double Sonnet for the Luna Moths

—Norton Island, Maine

For ten days now, two luna moths remain
silk-winged and lavish as a double broach
pinned beneath the porch light of my cabin.
Two of them, patinaed that sea-glass green
of copper weather vanes nosing the wind,
the sun-lit green of rockweed, the lichen's
green scabbing-over of the bouldered shore,
the plush green peat that carpets the island,
that hushes, sinks then holds a boot print
for days, and the sapling-green of new pines
sprouting through it. The miraculous green
origami of their wings—false eyed, doomed
and sensual as the mermaid's long green fins:
a green siren calling from the moonlight.

A green siren calling from the moonlight,
from the sweet gum leaves and paper birches
that shed, like tiny white decrees, scrolled bark.
They emerge from cocoons like greased hinges,
all pheromone and wing, instinct and flutter.
They rise, hardwired, driven, through the creaking
pine branches tufted with beard moss and fog.
Two luna moths flitting like exotic birds
towards only each other and light, in these
their final few days, they mate, then starving
they wait, inches apart, on my cabin wall
to die, to share fully each pure and burning
moment. They are, like desire itself, born
without mouths. What, if not this, is love?

The Plaza of Good Success

Your voice is a poem on fire in a wire birdcage.

Your voice is the black water over which yesterday watches tomorrow.

Your voice is the white water over which tomorrow watches yesterday.

Your voice fills my hair with metal filings, and each church I pass is a magnet that loves arches.

Your voice sleeps in my ear like the translucent egg of a wasp.

Your voice, when you cry, is the shadow of the aqueduct at noon.

Your voice, when you sing, is an aqueduct in which children are racing oranges.

Your voice is a two-foot fountain falling on itself.

Your voice can mend torn nets near the ocean.

Your voice falls like a broken moth.

Your voice rises like silver dust from a broken moth.

Your voice is the bulb, flower and light.

Your voice hums like the last page of a book.

Your voice, when you whisper promises, shatters the petals of the almond orchard.

Your voice is at once a naked girl waking and a woman undressing for bed.

Your voice comforts boys and paralyzes men. There is no in between.

Your voice is the mother of worth. She is great with child.

Your voice is the God of waves when you say goodbye.

Your voice never fills my bones enough, and this is why I am dying.

Your voice doubts because your voice has big eyes.

Your voice in a room angels with its muscles and feathers because it is the angel of the sun who vacations at the center of the sun.

Your voice is the voice of a woman singing with her eyes closed who mops concrete steps in an alley while she thinks of her favorite chapel in a great cathedral.

Your voice, the prayer of it, is God's birthday cake, and yes he will have a slice thank you.

Your voice likes to say *the plaza of good success.*

Your voice is the yellow-throated bird who sang to me in a park in Lisbon one fall, and I will know its name in many languages.

The Other Queen of Fado

Just enough sun on a soft black sweater,
she keeps the king standing at a gate
for hours while she wanders
at the pace of grazing sheep
El Greco green promontories.
The king is known for his overblown
suit of stone and the horse-head
she has convinced him to wear.
Her military is a silver cold front
flying a scabbardfish on its banner.
Hers is a kingdom of sheer cliffs
and sheets, and laundry day signals
a different kind of surrender.
When cold and sunny, she revels
in the solitude of chairs like the queen
of a bakery's late afternoon.
She meditates on an old earthquake,
or the dignity of ungainly storks
who have found poise in a thermal updraft,
mortally old cormorants warning,
by lifting missing feathers,
the fisherman heading out to sea
or passengers moving inland on a slow train,
sea snails writing their names and clutching
the dark curves of yuccas in cold weather,
the joy in the poverty of the Portuguese hat.
The masses know her smoke
by its almond oil and lavender,
and her walks favor white stone streets
that wind down to the beaches.
Her favorite toy is a child learning to smell.

She winds her up and lets her go
in a rose garden among hanging,
hand-tatted purses of flower teas.
What is her pet name for passion?
Reluctant luck. How does she entertain
the slow, cold bees of January?
She pours a glass of port.
How does she conquer her awe
of the fragrance of lavender?
She steeps it toward a tea.
She steps toward the sea.

ALYSE BENSEL

Where There Is Mystery, There Is a Woman

Why bear the weight of the prow
carved as you are, breasts bared
to the wind and salt, barnacles
clinging to your fins? I have begun
to worry about mermaids on ships
and on billboards, on television
shows and movies. The harshness
of the sun's glare. Pale as you all
are, do you burn when you emerge
from the ocean? Do your eyes sting
or, like a shark, never blink at all?
Even now, I watch the fading
as if you are a scar reluctant
to leave. We keep on dredging
you up, hunting whales whose singing
we will never understand. I am afraid
for you, for the chaffing of a seashell
bra Disney made you wear, for the neon
colored tails. I want you to keep
watching, barely seen, a flicker
of a tale or a splash receding.

Melusine Spinning Yarns

Who wouldn't think the French thought of mermaids
who gave advice to men who watched their fathers die,

who agreed to marriage if Saturdays they're off the hook
to be alone in the castle. Who lay by moonlit fountains.

Who, seeking revenge against their father, were punished
to spin as serpents. Who kept golden keys in their mouths,

itched to bathe in tiled bathtubs. Who, when caught, burst
into dragons. Who abandoned their children, as half-fish

often did. *Meluzina*: the wailing winds, the spawn
of the devil, the Lady of the Lake, those succubi who

appeared every seven years for the taking, who vanished
mourning for lost children they could no longer hold.

After the Flood the Captain of the Hamadryas *Discovers a Madonna*

He pulled everything he could save out of the water—
canoes snarled in tree roots, bruised mangoes,

cans of chilies, crates and crates of plantains splitting
from their tough yellowed skins—before he found her

upside down in a cecropia robed in mud and fish bones,
a woman's floral underwear wrapped around her feet.

He wiped the dirt from between her lips with a callused thumb
and felt what he dreaded—a godawful abundance of wonder.

Town after town, he towed the mother of God, but no one
would take her. One town said it lost a Christ with paint

flaking from his face. Another said they lost cattle to the river.
Another, a child. He offered the blooming peony panties

to every shaking head. For weeks, he rowed through storm
and sunstroke, promised her, *To God, the glory. To God, the power.*

To you the devotion of a penitent thief. But she remained unclaimed.
Macaws landed on her shoulders and sang whale songs.

When he cupped her smaller breast, he heard bells tolling
his own name. Morphos cloaked her at dusk, mated on her back

or slipped their proboscises, deep and tenderly, beneath her
blistered paint for the sweetness seeping from her warped hips.

One night as he passed a boat where men laughed as they threw rotting fish at caimans, her peeling cheeks smoothed, her splinters

lay back into the wood, her belly rounded against the robe, the child inside turning as it dreamed its own heartbeat. Then, he saw.

Then, he sorrowed. Then, the shameless, mortal awe as he cried, *For thine is the kingdom,* and rolled up his sleeves to deliver her.

The Fate of Maria José da Cruz's Seven Dolls

They arrive from America the day of the funeral,
      seams in their dresses unfinished, glue behind
   their eyes loosened by heat, blue gazes rattling

plastic heads, and the priest thinks, *Providence,*
      before giving them to the newly motherless girl.
   She dresses them in mourning, scolds them

as she brushes their hair while a capuchin steals one
      out of the cradle she made from a plantain crate.
   The one with the parted mouth she kisses

with the tip of her tongue until her father gives it away,
      knowing nothing of the one she buried after she broke
   her hymen on its hand. One, she tells her father,

was a mermaid's daughter who drowned but her body
      washed up where a handsome, young guitarist
   massaged her feet until her heart started.

Hers was a short-lived resurrection—his bruxa sister
      turned her into a doll. That's why, she explained,
   she cut it in half and tied it to a dead pacu—

so it could finally return to its mother. She nails one
      to a cross as a gift for the priest. She saws one open
   with a kitchen knife to see how girls are made and rubs

her finger along the smooth, hollowed shoulders and hips
        and thighs. One she dresses in mud and forgets it
    by the river. The tide takes it to a curious pirarucu,

and when the ribereño cuts into his boiled dinner's belly
        that night as he argues with his wife about the last time
    they made love during a full moon, a naked plastic girl spills

onto his table, slicked in blood and fish guts. *Ai Deus!* he cries,
        but it isn't God at all. *Ai Maria!* she cries, which is closer
    to the miracle born on their table. A single blue eye

crooked in its socket stares back. The wife grabs a stick
        and pushes the hard, unbreathing body back through
    the slit in the fish's belly. They'd asked for a son.

When I Go to Prison to Meet My Father

they bring a Spaniard with a glass eye and tattooed fingers.
He holds my hands across the table and tells me the story

of Iara, Our Maritime Lady of Gunpowder Kisses, who sang
to sailors until a red tide strangled out a song about a myrmidon

with a forked tail, a rattle for a tongue. I don't tell the guard
this isn't my father but offer the one-eyed prisoner consoling

fictions about the black cowboy boots embroidered with orchids
I found on a rooster's grave, about kites I flew over Guanabara Bay

engrafted with prayer, *Deliver us from bees colonizing the teapots.*
I imagine love, and then I feel it. I admit to planting crosses

in termite mounds, not—as the priest declared—to blaspheme
the Lord, but so they, too, might devour Christ and be saved.

He reopened the eyes of the murdered woman, not—
as the prosecution claimed—to steal them, but to sever her

from her sin so she might be promoted to glory. Police found
the bloody knife wrapped in her slip, but not her wallet,

or her dress, or the letter she wrote her son in São Paulo.
There is a moral happiness in the incestuous bellbird's lure.

Its hunger comes to tell us of a world elsewhere. A body in need,
then a needless body roused to dream the everlasting alone.

Sirena

to recount those five days/ fist nite/ first he picked her up
vomiting outside some village
bar / didn't finish inside her then / walked Central Park then 3
downtown to Times Esquare
& as walked several called hello Sirena / some called from Iraq &
she didn't answer / pues
then dinner in Little Italy & she felt happy to be away from her
deathly duties Sirena dancing
madly whipping her tail across the bar & scattering booze &
smashing glass

then made it at his chanti again before she fell asleep & she told
him come inside

next day . . . ¿did they drink?

can't remember

Sirena hear that gas burn
think they went to Alphabet City / rain / or maybe Empire State .
. . \
or that cd have been Friday /

Sat mermaid parade
long commute & we slept
then drank
& THUS commences that epic
or shd I begin in Vegas
as tribute to & confusion of Sirena . . .

her I begin w/ her b/c she's his

most seawardly love

wd you write that might have something of the everything that
makes the mother cry when she sleeps/ the
voices she hears the face she feels that taunts her/ estranges her
from her/ from what never really mattered to
any degree—what wd you write/ draw/ whatever—never. She
seemed to him to imposter danger.

Selkie

*The most common theme in selkie folklore, however, is one in
which a cunning young man acquires, either by trickery or theft, a
selkie-girl's sealskin.*

For years, you wore ordinary as a housecoat.
Typed memos by day and made weak

martinis by night. For years, you were the one
they could count on to sweep all the unsaid things

under the rug. Sometimes you're oblivious to blue.
Sometimes a shadow caught in a pool of light

makes you want to scratch off your skin,
dissolve in tides of wind that swing out and across

the street's moonlit lawns. Now, with your life
half gone, your child of amber eyes and ruby shoes

hands you what was nailed to the bottom
of a long-lost trunk. For six nights

you sleep on shore, cocooned in love's sheer
blanket. On the seventh you slip an arm

into fur that still glows like coals, feel
how this shell of warmth still holds

an echo of water's deep lullaby.
As you dive into a tango of stars, you turn

and watch her hand moving in adagio,
perfectly timed to the story you always told.

Epithalamion Doused with Moonshine

The dead don't bivouac by the riverside.
I reckon love ain't two fifths consolation,
but a pint of bastard light through the gut.
I reckon our dead congregate, reeling
past the pointy steeple of paradise.
Be my *Oh Susanna, don't you cry for—*,
and I'll be your banjo's clawhammer strum.
We'll mainline sawdust and speak, in shotgun,
the language of might coulds juked in the dark.
I love you like gingham loves knobby knees.
Love me like a holster loves a warm gun.
Let angels lead us away while the catfish
are still in bloom and while we still reckon
some drunk mermaid's hit us with her flipper.

KRISTY BOWEN

From *The Care and Feeding of Mermaids*

Forget what you know about women. About circumference. No one really loves the travel as much as they love the traveler. The sound of the foot at the door. She'll never have children, or bake, or know the constellations as well as you'd imagine. Her stories will keep you awake. How she and sister built castles from dixie cups and then obliterated them. How the water, the sky, was so blue it made her chest hurt. Forget what you know about memory. By day, she'll work in an office and write poems at her desk. Hypnotize herself to the clicking of fingers moving over keys, the subtle fluorescent flickering. Will learn to move about as if swimming, or better, to pretend to swim while treading water. She won't mention how she spends her lunch hour on the bathroom floor, tracing the grout with a finger nail and thinking about cities and structures. A perfect tower made of steel and concrete. How you could spend your whole life looking for the crack in the exterior and never even find it.

Don't worry about the bathtub, the bits of scale and hair caught in the drain, a little more each day. Only a fool would weather the storm at the northermost point. She'll still be good in bed. Adept at karaoke and drinking mai tais from glasses shaped like cats and dragons. Can probably name every crustacean by blind touch, her fingers seeking out each grooved exoskeleton in the dark. Warning: The vapor of her breath against the mirror will make you anxious. The way she winces over the sashimi and cries in the shower. At night, she'll slip out to meet men in hotel bars downtown, sneak into the pool after hours, call you at 3am begging for a ride home. Do not aquiesce. Especially on nights when the fog settles low on the water. Especially when the stars above it line up like a million tiny fish.

You must begin with white, but it's a dirty sort of white. Like the sound left after birds have alighted from the beach in a rush of feathers and noise. Seaglass is nice, something small and heart shaped, tiny enough to fit in the box under the bed. Never mind the whining and weaving she'll do with anything she can find: fishing line, seaweed, the plastic rings from soda cans. It's all very picturesque and quaint. Soon, the body will open with the slightest prodding, the scales glimmering in the sun. You must begin with language, but a dirty sort of language. Get her used to *cunt* and *fuck*. Soon she'll say them without the whisper. Soon you'll pull them from her throat like a string of pearls. Picture a water color in a turbine. What it's like for her on the inside. Leaking seascapes and an impossible father. It is foolish to love that which has freed you. Or that which you save. We know this, and yet, again we turn off the radio. Excite at the heft, the slightest shimmer in the net.

[the siren's story]

she wasn't born in this city. she found its basalt greenstone chunks, seafloor forced skyward. it found her hands through mist and odors whirring pigeons' clubfeet fluttering, toothless men's paper sacks spilling elixirs, roots, shark fin tonics. heat swelling sewer steam rising, side street chess match maneuvers mystifying. it sought her whirlwind hair, grown seavine thick. songbird, adrift, nestling neon, she crafted snares for moths, butterflies, treasure hunting children tracing ideographs: sky, sun. patina spires, smirking dragon boys humming silk lanterns, flight of phoenixes through fish vendors' stalls, corrugated plastic blackbird perches, jade-ringed gardens, needle-tipped shanties. it bulleted trees, lighting hash pipes; herbalists' storefront canopies concealing leathered men, versed in languages of whiskered ghosts. it invented her dialect carving tongue: salt fables, yellow caution tape palaces. she lost herself in this city. it lured her, drank her air; honey voice's precision, hybrid beyond memory. songbird, adrift, this city's misplaced siren. migration patterns subterranean streams swallowed whole.

Fish Store Mural Relocated

A splash of light on the gray bricks, the mermaid
lounges in a flowing, horizontal pose, her body—
breasts cuddled behind a forearm cross—twisting
so her sleepy eyes sweep the length of Lee Street.
She might have woken up on this block just in time
to see the skinny boy in T-shirt and huge sneakers
pay for a gun in the parking lot, glimpse the wheel-
chaired figure on the corner waving a sign that says
Vet Out of Work, Can Fix Anything. Long she
flourished here, brightening the dilapidated shops,

until the city felt the need to rescue her, brick
by brick, to a more prosperous side of Greensboro.
Her elegant tail, perfectly scaled, no longer waves,
but since the workers haven't reached her head, her
smile's unchanged. And though the coral lipstick's
cracked a bit, there's such an openness in her face
it's no wonder we want to lead her off to a place
untouched by roadside trash, where the homeless
won't huddle under her at night and let their dreams
trouble the quiet tide of her green hair.

Meditations on "Catch" by L. Hughes in Three Parts

I.

He carried a mermaid on a cart
full of splinters. "Hey, Big Boy,"

she teased, "God gave you lips,
use them as suction cups."

He sucked the sliver gently
from the scaly posterior.

II.

He stumbled with the mermaid
into the shack. "What's that?"

asked the wife. Big Boy wiped
the sweat from his forehead.

"God loves me," he mumbled,
"He loves me so good, He gave me

a sweet talkin' fish."

III.

Big Boy didn't go home
the following night. Away

from the waterfront, the wife
found a cart and an unzipped

tail tossed in the alley behind
the bin of the distillery.

Sea Oats

I soaked my oats. I soaked a merman
out of my oats. He must have been
dehydrated, disintegrated, vacuum-sealed.
With a honeyed finger I touched
his flesh. He purred. A thread of light
knotted my fingertip. A hummingbird
struck my window red. At my screen door
a pale deer chewed out her own heart.
In a kitchen like this, I couldn't tell
if I was sweating or if the ants had come
to crown me in a drippy swarm.
Never had my home pulsed so,
the Cuisinart sparking as the walls
danced their stuttering dance. I took
a fork to the merman's hair, took
it to my mouth. I could hear the squirrels
thrashing in the ventilation. To slurp
a merman from his pot, what finer
pleasure is there? He tasted
like a wafer, but to think of him
as a thing to be tasted was disgraceful.
I welcomed him wetly, my body
a jangle of parts rough-hewn.
I couldn't tell with my tongue
the divide between torso and tail:
He came to me as one wholesome form,
a cloud whipped into tornado.
I felt the foundation shift,
the sound of teeth against foam.

The Mermaid and the Siren

she   wears candy-floss wigs
irradiated bright
-er I experiment with vinegar
to clear the yellow wax
that brushes down to grease
along this straw that's sometimes ambergris,
            sometimes auburn and once
burning henna red

you'd think the ocean would fix us both
the magic keeps our tendrils dry

we grow
no blood
            so easy as thorns   in kelp

she has not been taken
            and I have not been loved

like clamshells   shattered   on the fish shit shore

Meliae

No one writes
        biographies of average mermaids
You know our lives
            by our exceptions
        tails sliced to legs
        by loss of voice or cloak   no- skin

You know us- foolish & afraid
            choosing cold ocean lovelies
    over warm-haired arms
                keep their damp inside
            at least for most of life

  you think
        but would not carry
these creatures born with scales
                that pinch skin between them
                and smell of other fish
        We've loved

Whoppers

The mermaids lied about Neverland. There was no boat, no ticking crock, just Hook and a band of lost boys. They lied about Atlantis, the sunken people, the city submerged, a bubbled civilization deep in a safe, blue abyss. They lied about cyclops, even in the depths of the sea there was no escape. Ahab lied. There was no whaler, no dick of Moby. Ahab was simply a dick. The old man in the sea, he lied. Not a marlin. Ariel lied. She wasn't mermaid or fish, just another voiceless woman with amnesia. Anyone would forget an event that turned every step into a feeling of knives.

Conspiracy Theory

The humans decide
to kill off the
mermaids. First they
catch them alongside
the accidental shark,
the stingray flailing,
the shredded
remnants of plastic
bags. *She was dead,*
they say, but chop off
her hair and give it to
their wives who braid
it into hairpieces,
wreaths, a corsage to
pin below the throat.
A chef in a high-end
restaurant in the
gentrified wing of the
meat district begins
offering mermaid
tail—first a one time
dish, then the Friday
night special, until it's
a regular choice below
blowfish and escargot.
Walmart carries
mermaid heart in
shrink-wrap on
styrofoam.
McDonalds offers

mermaid sandwiches with chunky tartar sauce. Hatcheries capture mermaid for breeding purposes and farms, feeding the demand for nymph battered and butter fried.

Rock Fight

The mermaids gather
rocks—small ones,
large ones. They drop
them into piles that
grow from the bottom
of the ocean. They
roll them between
fingers and thumb,
tuck them into their
hair, press them
against the curve of
their heart. The
mermaids throw rocks
at waves, watch
them drop, only to
catch them mid-fall
into darkness. They
like to feel where well
and sluice has made
them round, where
quartz edges scratch,
where pockmarks and
scars soften, rocks like
the faces of
adolescents, the jaws
of men, the underside
of what we drag as if
we could force pain
smooth. The
mermaids carry

stones—blue, specked,
misshapen,   glass.
They   despise
perfection,
symmetrical,   whole.
They   scour   the
beaches. They   dig
beneath   sunken
bellies of flotilla, fleet,
iceboat, yacht. They
take all they want.
They   seek   out
damage. They   want
mine.   They   want
yours.

From *Lost Boy Monologues*

—after *Peter Pan*, the stage play by J. M. Barrie

He hung that cobweb of a house around my neck like a chain, a necklace of cannonballs. Afraid I'd fly off. They clamored for stories: *Now the story you promised to tell us as soon as we were in bed!* I told them I'd no experience, but they didn't care. *Wendy, Lady, be our mother.* He wanted their thoughts tended too. Said he'd watched my mother do that at night while we slept: sorting the tangle, good from bad, putting the best on top where we'd look when we woke, like clothes in drawers, hiding *[shudders]* beneath.

He said *travel.* Said world. Said *adventure. There are mermaids.* The first boy who saw me tried to bury an arrow in my chest, and the *merfolk?!* Drown those who are not their kind. *How we should all respect you,* he lied. After that it was diapers & dinners/ flu & February/ babies & bathing & passing their time. I spun yarn after yarn after yarn—like yarn. He traveled. Said *pretend.*

When we left, he forgot us. Just like that. I'd promised to clean his house once a year, if he came back, which he did, only once. *Fancy forgetting the lost boys, even Captain Hook,* I said. *Tinker Bell?* he asked, *Who's that?*

Strings Concert: Sea Anemones

Working her
little mouth against
smooth glass, she beckons inaudible
to all the focused
faces that

stare straight stage
ward, row upon row
of intent parents, brows knit,
hands stiff; an occasional
chin lifts to

signal a
rhythm held, a se-
quence sinuously played, against con-
trary expectat-
tion. Beneath

her black net
tutu, her tight black
leotard, hangs the print underwear
worn by girls her age:
it might be

fish swimming
just above her round
thighs, or mermaids who whisper
what words she should say,
how to free us from

our frozen
stupor, trapped by violins that scrape
out the same choked notes,
dragging the jagged,
metal can

against a
concrete walk. What sea
rose grows at her center, between
arms
waving to us like
water plants?

What message
does she bring, drowned by
the pitching rhythms, first fast running
then tripped, hurled backward,
heavy, hard,

fighting for
balance, while she re-
turns again, again, again—twirling
and opening her mouth
to breathe out

bubbles that
appear and vanish
before they're ever seen, opening
and closing, invis-
ible trail.

After Leaving the Water on in the Upstairs Bathroom
or Warped Sonnet for a Mermaid

This morning an ocean poured through our vents
and we were floating away in our home.
My daughter and I tried to soak up what
we could, but the fountain continued to spill
over. When you arrived a tsunami
entered through your voice. Too many times I
have tried to be perfect, a painted wife,
portrait of a woman who could swim
through any undertow, who might lose her-
self underwater for a while, but who
always returns to the roll of the waves.
But today, I realized there were too
many fish in the aquarium, too
many leaks in the bottom of the sea.

Souvenir Boxes

If you think you are the mermaid, think again.
You are the ocean holding the mermaid afloat,
trying to change the world one dolphin at a time.

Even if it hurts, watch the sunrise.
Pico de gallo, pico de gallo. Salida del sol.

Bora Bora
= amazing.

We're so busy we forget
we're out of wine. Irony.
Headsnapper. Mad House-
wife. Raised by Wolves.

At first there were
whitecaps. Now?
Not enough water
to draw a bath.

Understand, it's never been easy to live,
when we're trying to escape ourselves.

I'm in a fever of doubt, so
you suggest I find my fan
club, wave from a balcony,
lower every expectation.

Maybe I'm still the mermaid.
Maybe the ocean is your hand.

I went to a psychic and her parrot
said, *You will eat the wild strawberries
on the dunes, then fall asleep.* I assumed

this meant a good life;
we were so hungry then.

I remember when our sea
of bathwater spilled onto
the bathmat, you spoke
to me in only washcloth:
backbone, backbone, breast.

Never enough,
said the parrot.

I am trying my best
to be your cocktail,
your emergency exit,
your whimsical kite.

Imagination is an echo chamber,
the parrot kept repeating.

Never mind
sometimes
we are lost.

On a Beach in Nova Scotia

Wait here for the sound of the tide. It might
be a while, for it is only about twice a month that you can
hear it from this hilltop. When the sun and the moon join
in a gravitational pull and tug the water up onto the shore
farther than usual. It is here that you might see
the elusive mermaid, drawn in over land normally closed
to her, camouflaged in the white spray, her hair like seaweed
torn from the rock, spread out around her, floating.
Here, for a few hours, you might glimpse her, if you look
with the right glint of determination in your eye.
You will not hear her sing, but experts say that is what
she is doing. You are most likely to see her if she feels
safe enough to lie on a rock and moonbathe. With binoculars,
you could see her gills, closed up against her neck
while she breathes air. Her eyes, if you could see them,
are the W-shaped irises of the cuttlefish, and her teeth, if she smiles,
are sharp and triangular, in rows. Her strangely human torso
is actually sharkskin-rough to the touch, glisten as it may
at this distance. The smooth, light gray torso gives way to
a darker, dappled tail. It shimmers: biologists claim that the mermaids
used those, once, as silent communication when hunting in shallow
waters during the day, or to confuse shoals of herring. But now,
this is the last confirmed mermaid. The lights from the cities
may have driven them away, or they may have been running
from eyes like yours. We do not know how they reproduced,
because since we discovered them, there has not been a new generation.
Now look away. Let the last mermaid enjoy her lonely beach.

Lago Cahuilla

There are no mermaids in the Salton Sea,
no siren's voices calling from the mist,
only a silence broken by small waves
almost unnoticed, lost against a sky
empty of native birds. The spirit craves
to know, at least nomadic wings persist
a moment at this edge, but even those

have disappeared. The sea and sky transpose
themselves, above, beneath, as if the air
were under water, and the currents held
by winds along the surface, where the dry
salt spray, or dust, lingers as if compelled
to hover an eternity. This spare
vision of unity consumes the sight

of anyone transfixed by woven light,
delighted, fascinated or enthralled
by these inversions, where the silence holds
dominion, understood as mute reply
to any questioning. Stillness enfolds
each phrase or canticle, whispered or called
from salt-choked voices, shibboleths: the same

angled contortions of a secret name.
And yet, if you accept the stillness, stay
as quiet as you can, silence your mind,
some say you'll hear migrations, wings so high
you cannot see them, but their song, refined
by light, can travel even through this gray
salt-crusted haze as soft epiphany.

The Extinction of the Mermaids

No evidence of aquatic humanoids has ever been found.
—The National Oceanic and Atmospheric Administration (2012)

Remember the timbers of the burning galleys
of the Trojans turning into the flesh & fin of green
daughters of the sea? They joined with the crones

inaccurately thought to have been cast for a scene
on the Romanian stage or out of Ireland by Saint
Patrick. This was GirlPower before the first waves

of feminism. They picked up Jullanar the Sea-girl
with eyes bordered with kohl & undulant hips,
skin smoother, the Arabs said, than the curved

inward surface of a conch. Another clutching comb
& mirror had unraveled her tail from a coat
of arms to join the ranks next to a Finnish Nakki

playing a silver harp o' night & the scaly daughter
of Ravana who had fallen in love with Hanuman.
Everyone followed the glinting jeweled fish shape

of Atargatis of Assyreia who had once made love
so fiercely that she suffocated her shepherd lover
to death & in mourning cast herself into the ocean

only to find her beauty too great to turn entirely
fish. One by one, they each joined the procession,
oscillating like a sine wave of charmed speech

& wriggling shanty. Men stood agape in front lawns,
mothers covered eyes of children, the word lurid
skipped on tips of lips. There was no Blackbeard

or Christopher Columbus to fight the premise.
No one seemed to remember their spawn
of eggs must have to be externally fertilized.

Their hair flowed in the sun, scales sapphire
as they moved together, a braid loosening over
the horizon, leaving behind a vestige of cruel

plunging happiness & the manatees. *Murduchu,*
murmured the sea. *Murduchu.* Just like that.
One after another. Then they were all gone.

NOTES ON CONTRIBUTORS

KELLI RUSSELL AGODON is the author of *Hourglass Museum, Letters from the Emily Dickinson Room, Small Knots,* and *Geography.* She co-edited the anthology *Fire On Her Tongue* and is the coauthor of *The Daily Poet: Day-By-Day Prompts For Your Writing Practice.* She cofounded Two Sylvias Press in Seattle. (www.agodon.com)

STEVEN ALVAREZ is an Assistant Professor of Writing, Rhetoric, and Digital Studies at the University of Kentucky. He is the author of *The Xicano Genome, The Pocho Codex,* and *Six Poems from the Codex Mojaodicus.* Read more of his work at www.stevenpaulalvarez.com.

ALYSE BENSEL is the Book Review Editor at *The Los Angeles Review* and Co-Editor of *Beecher's.* She is the author of the poetry chapbooks *Shift* (Plan B Press, 2012) and *Not of Their Own Making* (dancing girl press, forthcoming 2014). She is a PhD candidate in creative writing at the University of Kansas.

KRISTY BOWEN is a writer, visual artist, and the author of several chapbook, zine, and artists book projects; including the recent *Girl Show* (Black Lawrence Press, 2014) and *The Shared Properties of Water And Stars* (Noctuar Press, 2013). She runs dancing girl press & studio.

TRACI BRIMHALL is the author of *Our Lady of the Ruins* (W.W. Norton), winner the Barnard Women Poets Prize, and *Rookery* (SIU Press), winner of the Crab Orchard Series First Book Award. She's received an NEA Literature Fellowship and is an Assistant Professor of Creative Writing at Kansas State University.

DANTE DI STEFANO's poetry and essays have appeared recently in *The Writer's Chronicle, Shenandoah, Brilliant Corners, Obsidian,* and elsewhere. He was the winner of the Allen Ginsberg Poetry Award, the Ruth Stone Poetry Prize, The Phyllis-Smart Young Prize in Poetry, and an Academy of American Poets College Prize.

SUSAN J. ERICKSON lives in Bellingham, Washington, where she helped establish the Sue C. Boynton Poetry Walk and Contest. Her poems appear in *2River View, Crab Creek Review, Museum of Americana, The Fourth River, Hamilton Stone Review,* and *The Lyric* and in anthologies including *Malala: Poems for Malala Yousafzai.*

KATY E. ELLIS grew up under fir trees and high-voltage power lines in Renton, Washington. Aside from her chapbook *Urban Animal Expeditions* (Dancing Girl Press), her poetry appears in a number of literary journals in the U.S. and Canada. Currently, she teaches writing to home school children in West Seattle.

NATALIE FISHER was raised in Alabama and currently lives in Israel, where she is pursuing an M.A. in Creative Writing from Bar Ilan University. Her work is featured or forthcoming in *Museum of Americana, Blue Lyra Review,* and *Poetica Magazine.*

LISA PIERCE FLORES is an author (*The History of Puerto Rico*), journalist (*The New York Times, Entertainment Weekly*), essayist (*The Jewish Daily Forward*), and poet (*West Wind Review, Inkwell),* and writing teacher. Flores grew up in Lynchburg, Virginia, and began her writing career at *El Nuevo Pais,* a newspaper in Caracas, Venezuela.

M. BRETT GAFFNEY was born in Houston, Texas, holds an MFA in poetry from Southern Illinois University and is an associate editor for *Gingerbread House* literary magazine. Her poems have appeared or are forthcoming in *Exit 7, REAL, Still: the Journal, Licking River Review*, and *Permafrost*, among others.

QUINTON HALLETT writes and edits from Noti, Oregon. Active in the Oregon Poetry Association, she has co-hosted a reading series, facilitated poet visits to a rural high school, and served on the board. She has three chapbooks, and her full-length poetry collection *Mrs. Schrödinger's Breast* is forthcoming from Uttered Chaos.

EMILY LAKE HANSEN is the author of the chapbook *The Way the Body Had to Travel* (dancing girl press, 2014). Her poetry has appeared in *Atticus Review* and *Dressing Room Poetry Journal* among others. She received an MFA from Georgia College & State University and currently teaches in Atlanta.

MATTHEA HARVEY is the author of five books of poetry—*If the Tabloids are True What Are You?, Of Lamb* (an illustrated erasure with images by Amy Jean Porter), *Modern Life* (a finalist for the National Book Critics Circle Award and a New York Times Notable Book), *Sad Little Breathing Machine*, and *Pity the Bathtub Its Forced Embrace of the Human Form*. She has also published two children's books, *Cecil the Pet Glacier*, illustrated by Giselle Potter and *The Little General and the Giant Snowflake*, illustrated by Elizabeth Zechel. She teaches poetry at Sarah Lawrence and lives in Brooklyn.

REBECCA HAZELTON is the author of *Fair Copy* (Ohio State University Press, 2012) and *Vow* (Cleveland State University Press, 2013). Her poems have been published in *Poetry, Best American Poetry 2013, Smartish Pace*, and *AGNI*.

DANIEL HEFFNER graduated with an MA in poetry from the University of North Texas in 2013. He has been a volunteer reader for the *American Literary Review* and is currently the audio-video director for the Kraken Reading Series in Denton, TX, as well as a reviewer for *American Microreviews and Interviews.*

LORI LAMOTHE's first poetry book, *Trace Elements*, is forthcoming from Kelsay Books. She has also written several chapbooks, including *Ouija in Suburbia* (dancing girl press, 2014) and *Diary in Irregular Ink* (ELJ Publications). Her poems have appeared in *Alaska Quarterly Review, Blackbird, CALYX, Wicked Alice* and elsewhere.

W.F. LANTRY, a native of San Diego, has two poetry collections: *The Structure of Desire* (Little Red Tree 2012), winner of a 2013 Nautilus Award in Poetry, and *The Language of Birds* (Finishing Line Press 2011). Recent honors: *Potomac Review, Old Red Kimono, Crucible* and *Cutbank* Poetry Prizes. He currently lives in Washington D.C. and is a contributing editor of *JMWW.*

HEATHER LYN is the author of *Café Con Voodoo.* Along with published poems and shorts, her play, "Shangri-La" placed second in the Agnes Scott Writer's Festival. She will have a horror fiction piece in an upcoming Anthology *From Dusk 'til Dawn*, and is currently finishing her second novel.

SHAHÉ MANKERIAN's most recent manuscript, *History of Forgetfulness*, has been a finalist at two prestigious contests: the 2013 Crab Orchard Series in Poetry Open Competition and the Bibby First Book Competition. His poems have appeared in *Mizna.*

SEAN NEVIN is the author of *Oblivio Gate* (Southern Illinois University Press) and *A House That Falls* (Slapering Hol Press).

His honors include a Literature Fellowship in Poetry from the National Endowment for the Arts, the Robinson Jeffers Tor House Prize for Poetry, the Alsop Review Poetry Prize, the Katherine C. Turner Academy of American Poets University Prize, and two fellowships from the Arizona Commission on the Arts. His poetry has appeared in numerous journals including *The Gettysburg Review, North American Review,* and *JAMA.*

MARTIN OTT is the author of four books of poetry: *Underdays* (Notre Dame University Press, 2015), *Captive* (C&R Press, 2012), and *Poets' Guide to America,* as well as *Yankee Broadcast Network* (Brooklyn Arts Press, 2014), co-authored with John F. Buckley. In 2013, he published *The Interrogator's Notebook,* Story Merchant Books. Blogs at writeliving.wordpress.com

JOHN POCH has published four collections of poems. His most recent, *Fix Quiet,* won the 2014 New Criterion Poetry Prize. He is director of the creative writing program at TTU and has poems recently in *The Nation, Poetry, Southwest Review,* and *New England Review.*

CHRISTINA M. RAU is the author of the chapbook *For The Girls, I* (Dancing Girl Press, 2014) and founder of the Long Island reading circuit Poets In Nassau. She teaches English at Nassau Community College where she also serves as Editor for The Nassau Review and Coordinator for the Creative Writing Project. Her poetry has most recently appeared in the journals *Technoculture, Crony,* and *Redheaded Stepchild.* In her non-writing life, she practices yoga occasionally and line dances on other occasions. Find her links on http://alifeofwe.blogspot.com.

BARBARA JANE REYES' most recent collection of poetry is *Diwata* (BOA Editions, Ltd., 2010). Her first book, *Gravities of Center,* was published by Arkipelago Books (San Francisco) in

2003, and her second book, *poeta en san francisco* (Tinfish Press, Kaneohe, Hawai'i) received the 2005 James Laughlin Award from the Academy of American Poets.

DAN ROSENBERG is the author of *The Crushing Organ* (Dream Horse Press, 2012) and *cadabra* (Carnegie Mellon University Press, 2015). His work has won the American Poetry Journal Book Prize and the Omnidawn Poetry Chapbook Contest. Rosenberg earned an M.F.A. from the Iowa Writers' Workshop and a Ph.D. from The University of Georgia. He teaches literature and creative writing at Wells College and co-edits Transom.

JENNY SADRE-ORAFAI is the author of four chapbooks and the collection *Paper, Cotton, Leather.* She is co-founding editor of *Josephine Quarterly* and Associate Professor of English at Kennesaw State University.

RAVI SHANKAR is the founding editor and Executive Director of *Drunken Boat,* one of the world's oldest electronic journals of the arts. He has published or edited seven books and chapbooks of poetry, including the 2010 National Poetry Review Prize winner, *Deepening Groove.* Along with Tina Chang and Nathalie Handal, he edited W.W. Norton's *Language for a New Century: Contemporary Poetry from Asia, the Middle East & Beyond.* He is an Associate Professor of English at CCSU.

MARK SMITH-SOTO is an associate editor of *International Poetry Review.* His poetry has appeared in *Antioch Review, Kenyon Review, Literary Review, Nimrod, Rattle, The Sun,* and other publications. The most recent of his eight books are *Berkeley Prelude: A Lyrical Memoir* (Unicorn Press, 2012) and *Time Pieces* (Main Street Rag Publishing Co., 2015).

MELISSA STEIN is the author of the poetry collection *Rough Honey,* winner of the 2010 APR/Honickman First Book Prize. Her work has appeared in *Southern Review, Harvard Review, New England Review, Best New Poets,* and many other journals and anthologies. She is a freelance editor and writer in San Francisco. (www.melissastein.com)

ELIZABETH KATE SWITAJ teaches literature, creative writing, and composition at the College of the Marshall Islands, on a coral atoll in Micronesia. She is a Contributing Editor to *Poets' Quarterly.* Her poems have recently appeared in *Red Savina Review, Clare Literary Journal*, and *Really System.* For more information, visit www.elizabethkateswitaj.net.

CAITLIN THOMSON resides in the Chuckanut Mountains. Her work has appeared in numerous places, including *The Literary Review of Canada, The Alarmist*, and the anthology *Killer Verse.* Her second chapbook, *Incident Reports,* is forthcoming in 2014 from Hyacinth Girl Press. You can learn more about her writing at www.caitlinthomson.com.

WENDY VARDAMAN (wendyvardaman.com, @wendylvardaman) is the author of *Obstructed View* and *Reliquary of Debt* (Lit Fest Press), co-editor/webmaster of *Verse Wisconsin,* and co-founder of Cowfeather Press. She is one of Madison, Wisconsin's two Poets Laureate (2012-2015) and co-editor of *Echolocations, Poets Map Madison.* In addition to poetry and flash prose, she writes essays, reviews, and interviews.

ASHLEY WARNER studies English at the University of West Georgia. She has received scholarships to attend the New York State Summer Writers' Institute and the Sewanee Writers' Conference.

JULY WESTHALE is a Pushcart and Fulbright-nominated writer based out of Oakland, CA. She has been awarded residencies from the Lambda Literary Foundation, Napa Valley, Tin House and Bread Loaf. Her poetry has most recently been published in *Adrienne, burntdistrict, Eleven Eleven, WordRiot, 580 Split, Quarterly West*, and *PRISM International.* She is the 2014 Poetry Fellow at Tomales Bay. (www.julywesthale.com)

LAURA MADELINE WISEMAN is the author of more than a dozen books and chapbooks and the editor of *Women Write Resistance: Poets Resist Gender Violence.* She holds a doctorate from the University of Nebraska and has received an Academy of American Poets Award and the Wurlitzer Foundation Fellowship.

REPRINT CREDITS

Kelli Russell Agodon: "Souvenir Boxes," *Hourglass Museum* (White Pine Press, 2014). Reprinted by permission of the author.

Alyse Bensel: "Where There Is Mystery, There Is A Woman" and "Melusine Spinning Yarns," *Not of Their Own Making* (Dancing Girl Press, 2014). Reprinted by permission of the author.

Kristy Bowen: "From *The Care and Feeding of Mermaids,*" (all three pieces) *Stirring: A Literary Collection.* Reprinted by permission of the author.

Traci Brimhall: "*After the Flood the Captain of* the Hamadryas Discovers a Madonna," *Passages North.* "*The Fate of Maria Jose da Cruz's Seven Dolls,*" *Hayden's Ferry Review.* "*When I Go to Prison to Meet My Father,*" *Gulf Coast.* Reprinted by permission of the author.

Dante Di Stefano: "Epithalmion Doused with Moonshine," *HUNGER Mountain.* Reprinted by permission of the author.

Katy E. Ellis: "The Wedding of Cecyl and Otter," *The Fiddlehead: Atlantic Canada's International Literary Journal,* 2000. Reprinted by permission of the author.

Rebecca Hazelton: "[At last, to be identified]," *The Journal.* Reprinted by permission of the author.

Lori Lamothe: "Selkie," *Bolts of Skin.* Reprinted by permission of the author.

Sean Nevin: "Hinged Double Sonnet for Luna Moths," *Oblivio Gate*. (Southern Illinois University Press, 2008). Reprinted by permission of the author.

Barbara Jane Reyes: "[the siren's song]," *Poeta en San Francisco.* (Tinfish, 2005), and *Nocturnes 3: (Re) View of the Literary Arts* (2004). Reprinted by permission of the author.

Dan Rosenberg: "Sea Oats," *Unstuck*. Reprinted by permission of the author.

Mark Smith-Soto: "Fish Store Mural Relocated," *North Carolina Literary Review*. Reprinted by permission of the author.

Melissa Stein: "Pantoum," *Gulf Coast* and *Rough Honey* (APR/Copper Canyon Press, 2010). Reprinted by permission of the author.

Elizabeth Kate Switaji: "Meliae" *Magdalene & The Mermaids* (Paper Kite Press, 2009). Reprinted by permission of the author.

Wendy Vardaman: "From *Lost Boy Monologues*," composed for the *Encyclopedia Show* and first appeared in *Mixtini Matrix*. Reprinted by permission of the author.

Laura Madeline Wiseman: "Whoppers," *Smoking Glue Gun*, Issue 7, 2013. "Conspiracy Theory," *Popcorn Farm*, 2014. "Rock Fight," *Goblin Fruit*, 2014. All three poems also appear in *Spindrift* (dancing girl press, 2014).

ABOUT THE EDITOR

Trista Edwards is an Ohio born, Georgia Peach living it up in Texas. She currently serves as the Reviews Editor at *American Literary Review,* as well as Co-Director of Kraken, an independent poetry reading series in Denton, Texas. A graduate of the University of West Georgia, Trista is currently a Doctoral Fellow in English at the University of North Texas. Her poems and reviews are published or forthcoming in *The Journal, Mid-American Review, 32 Poems, American Literary Review, Stirring: A Literary Collection, Birmingham Poetry Review, The Rumpus, Sout'wester, Moon City Review,* and more. It probably goes without saying, but her obsession with mermaids has been lifelong.

OTHER SUNDRESS PUBLICATIONS TITLES

major characters in minor films
Kristy Bowen
ISBN 978-1939675-19-4
$14.00

Confluence
Sandra Marchetti
ISBN 978-1939675-16-3
 $14.00

Hallelujah for the Ghosties
Melanie Jordan
ISBN 978-1939675-15-6
$14.00

Fortress
Kristina Marie Darling
ISBN 978-1939675-13-2
$14.00

When I Wake It Will Be Forever
Virginia Smith Rice
ISBN 978-1939675-10-1
$14.00

The Lost Animals
David Cazden
ISBN 978-1939675-07-1
$14.00

A House of Many Windows
Donna Vorreyer
ISBN 978-1939675-05-7
$14.00

The Hardship Post
Jehanne Dubrow
ISBN 978-0977089-26-0
$14.00

The Old Cities
Marcel Brouwers
ISBN 978-0972322-49-2
$14.00

One Perfect Bird
Letitia Trent
ISBN 978-0972322-48-5
$14.00

Like a Fish
Daniel Crocker
ISBN 978-0972322-47-7
$14.00

The Bone Folders
T.A. Noonan
ISBN 978-1939675-11-8
$14.00